THINK
LIKE A
CHAMPION

AND

Win!

Experience Major Breakthroughs & Progressive Successes

THINK
LIKE A
CHAMPION

AND

Win!

Personal Advisor. Master Coach. Motivational Speaker.

Dr. Clarice Fluitt

THINK LIKE A CHAMPION AND WIN!

Experience Major Breakthroughs & Progressive Successes

Published by Clarice Fluitt Enterprises, LLC

Printed in the USA

Cover Design & Interior Layout: www.wendykwalters.com

ISBN (print) : 978-0-9903694-7-9

To contact the author:

Clarice Fluitt | P.O. Box 15111 | Monroe, LA 71207

WWW.CLARICEFLUITT.COM
WWW.REALRESULTS.SOLUTIONS

TABLE OF CONTENTS

YOUR MOST
UNIQUE
SELF

I believe today is going to be one of the most outstanding days that you have ever had. I believe that your attitude is filled with gratitude and that you are on fire, ignited, excited, and delighted to be alive. Never has there been a day like today—so, make the best of this day as you go. Begin to open your mouth, look at yourself, and say, "WOW! I am a one-time-only creation of God. When He made me He said, 'That is a signed, sealed, original.'"

With this attitude—that you are a head, above, blessed, empowered, and loved by God—you are positioned to be a carrier of incredible life wherever you go.

I AM A ONE-TIME-ORIGINAL CREATION OF GOD

UNDERSTANDING OUR PERSONAL BLUEPRINT

Understanding our personal blueprint and how we have been created is important; what causes us to think, act, and behave the way we do. Through the examination of this, we learn how to create lasting changes and complete what we start through the process of discovering, understanding, and aligning our internal drive to move in the direction that we desire to move in; a direction that serves not only me, but all those that we care about. Get focused. Get a strategy. Take action.

WE LEARN HOW TO CREATE LASTING CHANGES AND COMPLETE WHAT WE START THROUGH THE PROCESS OF DISCOVERY AND DISCIPLINE

CHANGING LIMITING BELIEFS

There are ways to find out how you can change any limiting beliefs that you might have and what forces are shaping your life. The path to changing limiting beliefs begins with being able to identify the ABCs of faith and success.

A. **Get focused**

B. **Get a good strategy**

C. **Take action**

Clarify the results that you desire. Make it clear and identify what is really important to you; not what is important to your mother, father, husband or wife, kids, and friends. Back up and get in touch with yourself. Start by learning to love yourself. Until we love ourselves, we do not have the power to love others because other people's success tends to bring condemnation and make us feel unworthy or jealous.

CLARIFY THE RESULTS THAT YOU DESIRE

WHAT SHAPES
A DESTINY?

I am so excited about the power of decision. We are able to exercise emotional fitness and psychological strength that takes us to action. Nothing changes without new action. It is essential to remember that every action is parented by a decision. Before you can have an action, you have to make a decision. No matter how inconsequential it may seem, the smallest decision can literally change the outcome of your life. It is in your moment of decision that destiny is shaped.

NOTHING CHANGES WITHOUT NEW ACTION

THE FUEL THAT CHANGES YOUR MIND

Two incredible things in our lives I want to talk about are achievement and fulfillment. I have found that these are totally different from each other. Achievement is going from where we are to where we want to be and requires a plan and specific strategy.

With regard to fulfillment, I have the opportunity as an inspirational and motivational speaker to meet some fabulous people; many of whom are incredibly wealthy. Many times, people that have more money than they know what to do with are not happy; not fulfilled. They have great achievements in their lives, but many do not know who they are or where they are going. If we erroneously think that money will make us happy, it is more important to find out what we have been created for and where we belong.

The fuel that we need are mentors, coaches, and people to help us with this process. Whether we want to improve our financial outlook, or enhance our relationships, or fix our body there is a set of Scriptural and scientific principles that guarantee results.

PERSISTENCE

When you reach a point where it seems like you cannot figure out a solution, that is when the illusion of failure will keep you from reaching your goals. In reality, if you feel strongly enough about something, no amount of time or perceived lack of resources will keep you from achieving what you believe. The potential is there. That is called limitless thinking.

DO NOT FALL FOR THE ILLUSION OF FAILURE ... POTENTIAL IS THERE!

A
NEW
SEASON

Years ago, I was very interested in learning how to be a real estate agent. It seemed to be very complicated. I had to learn about everything that was entailed in real estate; there was so much to master. My husband was a real estate broker. He was going to teach me all I needed to know. That lasted about as long as a snowball in purgatory because I did not respond to the familiar. I had to hire someone that I could hear.

Hear what your teachers are saying to you. If you are really interested in increasing your knowledge, your opportunities, you will find that avenues of revenue are knocking at your door. It's the season, it's time to explore. It may be a little rhyme, but it's just in time. You have been called to greatness. You have been created to do things that are wonderful and that will bring increase not only to your life but to other people as well.

By the way, I did embrace the procedure and became a very successful real estate agent.

CREATED
TO MAKE
A DIFFERENCE

Your emotions filter what you do and trigger the action, whether good or bad. They will sometimes also trigger non-action and cause you to put yourself in self-imposed time out. When you are fearful, worried, angry, or stressed, you will act differently than when you feel determined, happy, or playful. Choose to determine what you want to achieve.

At 72 years of age, after preaching for over 40 years, I started a new career. It seemed like an impossible thing for me; but, I am doing it, doing it well, and using it to encourage you. What will you do to go to a higher level?

DETERMINE WHAT YOU WANT TO ACHIEVE

DON'T RUN YOUR DAY ON AN EMPTY TANK

When I wake up in the morning I find that the first thing I have to do is make a decision as to which one of me is going to get up and face the day; the positive me, or the negative me? I have to choose. We are a people making choices with our voices.

Life draws life, so decide today that all the things around you are going to be positive. You choose positive things and bring them to you through the way that you think, speak, and act; thoughts, words, and deeds. Remember, not to decide is a decision.

Passion is like dynamite. It expands into your thoughts, actions, words, and the way you interact with people. The moment you open your eyes in the morning, rather than allowing a negative thought, bring order to your thought life. Your thoughts and words lead to actions. Say with your mouth that you are happy, that you feel good, that you feel great. Learn to encourage and strengthen yourself. If the devil can get your joy, he can get your healing, deliverance, prosperity, and relationships.

Instead of thinking that you do not have enough time or money, don't know the right people, or have the training or education (which may all be a fact) understand that those thoughts are not truth.

All the resources, or lack thereof, are not your problem; your mouth is your problem. If you keep saying you cannot have it, cannot get it, or are limited, change your mouth. If you say you do not have the right or enough education, through the internet you can learn almost anything you set your mind to. If the obstacle seems impenetrable, get focused and find another way. Be determined, flexible, creative and look for money, talents, gifts, and abilities to come your way. Say the right things. Feel good about yourself.

THERE'S MORE TO ME THAN WHAT YOU MIGHT SEE!

A
POSITION
OF REST

Something that I have learned over these many years is the importance of rest. We talk about an increase in money, time, talent, and treasure, but you also need to know how to have an increase of doing everything from a position of rest. It is so significant. I really believe God's best is a people at rest; not always trying to achieve but simply coming to a place where, according to the Word of God, all your cares are cast on Him because He cares for you.

I find it very relaxing to me that I can get a good hot cup of coffee, sit on my wonderful couch with my 2 little doggies sitting next to me, and the next thing I know revelation and inspiration comes. I begin to restore myself by resting. Resting is a decision. You have to be in charge of creating your own atmosphere that will be conducive for rest and will allow you to hear your own heartbeat.

RESTORATION

I found that restoration is not just the repair of something; to restore something is to make it better than it was originally. I want to encourage you to take your body, soul, and spirit into times of restoration.

Get away from all the other voices that are talking when nobody's there but you; the voices that keep reminding you to do this, and do that, or you didn't do this, and you didn't do that. Make those voices be silent by setting your affections on things that are above and not beneath. Just simply say with your mouth, "This is my time for restoration. I am not just resting my physical body, but my body, soul, and spirit. My triune being has just come to sit, recuperate, and restore."

THIS IS MY TIME FOR RESTORATION

LEGITIMATE QUESTIONS THAT PROVOKE THOUGHT

Have you ever thought about what you think about? There is an adage that says the mind is a terrible thing to waste. When we think about what we think about, it seems as though there might be an entire room in our mind filled with questions we have asked in the past. These might have produced nothing in the sense that we could apply the answer to our lives. Perhaps the questions are still lying dormant and unresolved.

It has been my experience that a natural outcome of thinking about what you think about is a deeper dimension of thought that results in the provocation of questions leading to answers that are applicable; that we can actually do something with. These answers will not only benefit us, but also enrich the lives of everyone around us. Practice thinking about what you think about and see where it takes you.

You might find yourself pleasantly surprised at the answers that come from legitimate, full, enterprising thought-provoking questions.

NEW
BEGINNINGS

Opportunities are all around in the areas of finances, relationships, attitudes, health, well-being encouraging you to come to the place of recognizing your own potential. I believe there are those of you reading this today that may be thinking you need to take a course on new beginnings. You need to clean out your mental closet. I have found that you can make all kinds of decisions, but that does not mean anything actually transpired from the thought. It doesn't necessarily mean you got your closet cleaned out just because you made a decision.

I want to encourage you to write down the steps you are going to take once you have made a decision to move in a positive forward direction. If you decide to lose weight, take a new class, sign up for life coaching, whenever you make that decision, make a positive move in that direction so you can begin to disconnect from the things that have been familiar. Do not try to do something new by embracing the old way that you used to do it.

NOT TO DECIDE IS A DECISION

These are some things I have found that really hinder us from embracing change. When you begin to say to yourself that you don't feel like doing this, or doing that, remember this: the way you feel begins with what you are focusing on. Choose to focus on things that are lovely, pure, true, and good. If your brain begins to think about how hard something will be to do, or that something you were going to do is not worth the effort, you will talk yourself out of doing the thing that will be meaningful to your life and produce your desired change.

Not to decide is a decision. Recognize when you have begun to postpone making a decision or excuse yourself from doing what you know you are supposed to do. Once you make a decision, begin to move in that direction.

STOPS
AND
STARTS

With every clear and compelling vision that you have, make a plan and develop a strategy that will fit in with it. If, for instance, your goal is to lose 20 pounds, or take a Bible class, or get a life coach—whatever your goal is, write it down. It must be compelling to you. Sometimes we have to get some help with these things.

I recently had to change my diet. Initially, I found it to be a stop and start, and stop and start pattern. I found that I needed encouragement along the way and a strategy, which meant that I needed a helper in the form of a mentor, coach, trainer, or teacher that would encourage, exhort, edify, build up and hold me accountable.

Once you have made a decision, have a plan written out, and obtained some help with all of this, immediately take action. Do not wait. Keep in mind that a decision should go with a commitment. Proper alignment will determine the success of your assignment. Align yourself with your dream; the vision. Commit to it and invest in yourself. Begin to celebrate where you are going and what you are doing.

REAL
CHANGE

If you really want change, not just a rearrange, but real change in your life, you must begin to pay close attention to the words that you repeat to yourself. You cannot continually tell yourself that you are getting old and forgetful, or that you can hardly get up and down. Be careful of the words you repeat to yourself because your words carry life or death and will draw to you whatever you say.

If you want to change your life, remember to pay attention to the words that you are saying about yourself. These words can change the way you feel. If you feel like a loser, you will act like one. If you feel like a winner and tell yourself you can do whatever your desire is; if you make no excuses when something looks hard and challenging, you take it one step at a time. If you fall off the horse, get up and get back on it!

POSITIVE OUTCOME

I recently did a 21-day de-toxification where you could only eat salad and everything had to be organic. I thought I would die eating nothing but salad and got to the point where I did not want to take another bite of it, but I made it through. The amazing thing was that I felt so much better. I decided this was going to be my lifestyle until my brain got into it and convinced me it would be too hard and too confusing to do. My brain told me I would have to be too disciplined to do this and did not have the time.

Just because you tried something once and did not do it right the first time does not mean you are going to be a failure forever. Even with me, I will do it over and over and over again until my brain says it will agree with me. My brain is not going to be in charge of me.

Empower yourself with the words that you say by choosing to focus on a positive outcome. Change how you feel and look for pleasure in the things that you embrace.

GOING
TO THE
NEXT LEVEL

What is your definition of what you would consider necessary to take your life to the next level? When you think you have hit a wall, remember, it is not a wall, it is a call to go to the next level. The things, the tools, the gifts ... unproductive and energy draining relationships; trade them all in for a whole new area of understanding.

YOUR WALL IS NOT A WALL
IT IS YOUR CALL!

LEARNING
NEW WAYS

Many of us have settled and limited our opportunities by telling ourselves that this is as far as we can go. By saying this, we have relegated ourselves to the back of the bus, financial ruin, and broken-heartedness.

If we want to go to another level, there are things that we need to detach from in order to embrace new ways of doing business.

WHAT DO I NEED TO DETACH FROM IN ORDER TO ADVANCE?

DETERMINE WHAT YOU WANT TO ACHIEVE

You determine what you want to achieve by deciding where your focus is going to be. If you are focusing on twenty different things, you will not do any of those things effectively. You may be able to do all twenty in your lifetime, but you will never be able to do all twenty at the same time.

1. Decide what you want.

2. Consciously choose what you want.

3. Do not focus on what you fear because God did not give you a spirit of fear.

4. Your dreams come alive when you meditate on them, talk about them, and chew on them day and night.

5. Recognize and focus on the opportunities that are coming to you.

6. Do not think about the things you have missed. If something did not work the first time, get up, you are a different person today than you were then.

7. Feed your brain good thoughts and refuse to let it wander.

These are seven points that will help you determine what you want to achieve once you have acknowledged what is important to you; who you are, where you are going, and how you are going to get there. Where your focus goes, your energy flows.

WHERE YOUR FOCUS GOES YOUR ENERGY FLOWS

BELIEVE
IN YOURSELF

Begin to make a list of your dreams and thoughts. This is not a wish list or pipe dreams, but a list of the things you desire to see an increase in by setting goals and positioning yourself so that opportunities are not missed. I heard someone say to me one time that they had an opportunity come into their life in their senior years. Then, somebody told them they were too old to make it work. Needless to say, they got very discouraged. I said to them, "You know, if you're going to believe in yourself, then you have to stay away from people who are always going to be telling you why you can't do something."

My advice to all of you who desire to see increase in your life is to find people who celebrate you, not just tolerate you. Find people who encourage you and build you up.

If you find yourself having a hard time finding the kind of people who celebrate you, perhaps you need to turn loose of some of the negative people and make a decision. Think of things that you have a passion about. See every idea, thought, concept, course, whatever it is, as an opportunity and go with it.

LIVE YOUR LIFE
WITH HAPPINESS
AND HARMONY

I make declarations over myself all the time and give thanks to God who always causes me to triumph in every situation. I look in the mirror and tell myself that I know I am the apple of God's eye, I know that He loves me from the top of my head to the souls of my feet, and I refuse to give in to the negative. Tell yourself that every day in every way you are getting stronger and lasting longer.

Saying positive things about yourself is not being conceited. Day by day you will begin to live your life with happiness and harmony.

It is time to love yourself and have some fun.

I KNOW THAT I AM THE APPLE OF GOD'S EYE

YOUR
REALITY

When I was a child, I heard my aunt say to my mother that I have an olive complexion. The only olive I had ever seen was green. I looked at myself in the mirror and asked myself if I was really green. I did not know that what it really meant was that I had a tanned complexion. For years and years, the thought came to me that when people looked at me I looked green to them. I allowed that comment of being green to become a fear of being around people. My aunt was not trying to put me down. I took her words apart from the spirit in which she was speaking based on my incomplete knowledge. I put that into my little brain computer and came up with the wrong thing.

There are things you have heard that people have said about you. It does not make it true just because someone said something or tried to tell you that you could not do this or that. If you have a sincere desire, if you really want to determine what you want to achieve, make a decision and choose to focus on a positive outcome. The meaning your brain gives to the situation, whether it is pain or pleasure, whatever meaning your brain gives to the experience, will make it your reality.

WORDS OF ENCOURAGEMENT

Regardless of the situation that you are confronted with, you can win. I have heard it said that there are overcomers in this world. The circumstances that you are confronted with are an invitation saying you cannot stay where you are. Maintain an attitude toward embracing change where you see yourself as an overcomer. Tell yourself that you can win and consider your circumstances as an invitation to the next level.

CONSIDER YOUR CIRCUMSTANCES AS AN INVITATION TO THE NEXT LEVEL

TAKE CHARGE

Anything in life that you *really* want is usually because you believe it will make life better for you, and it is a good feeling. When you feel good, you act differently. When you go through physical or mental discomfort and relief comes, it creates a deeper appreciation.

Emotion is created by a motion. Whatever you are feeling is related to how you are using your body. You feel better about things when you take care of your body. For example, if you are at your computer for a very long time, your arms hurt, your eyes are strained, and your body begins to get tired. Your physical body needs to move, walk, and get some fresh air every now and then.

Get in charge of your emotions before emotions get in charge of you.

EMOTION IS CREATED BY A MOTION

THE
BLAME GAME

Do not waste your sorrow or begin to blame people or situations. Blaming an event can be convenient because it helps preserve an identity that tries to shield you from true fear; the fear of failure, of not being loved or accepted. I am a victim of an event. It is always someone else's fault. There is nothing wrong with me, it was the other person. There is nothing I need to change. That thinking will limit you from accomplishing your full potential and put you into the prison of being a very limited person.

One of the worst things you can do is blame yourself. Most people think that this is being responsible and carries the connotation of humility. The situations and circumstances might say you are oppressed, lonely, and messed up; but, the Word of God says you are healed, delivered, and prosperous. Blaming yourself will never make anything better. Learn to embrace change, and learn from every life experience.

RECOGNIZING OPPORTUNITIES

Do not cry over spilled milk. Get out of pining over the things that you did not do and begin to acknowledge that with God, all things are possible. Get excited about that! Do not get caught in yesterday and miss out on the now. Opportunities are all around you so learn to look for them.

The next time the curtain goes up, do not miss your curtain call. Focus on the opportunities that are coming to you and learn to recognize them as opportunities. It is as though you are in a play and have a cue to make your entrance at a particular time, but you get preoccupied and miss your opportunity. The curtain goes up, and the curtain comes down. The good news is the curtain will go up again and you will get another opportunity.

DO NOT GET CAUGHT IN YESTERDAY AND MISS OUT ON THE NOW

INVESTING
IN
YOURSELF

I have five children. When they were all young and at home, we would get around the table at the end of the day so they could do their homework. I would think I was going to help them and would say to my daughter, "Let me show you how this works. You're learning how to do your addition, like 2 apples and 2 apples equals 4 apples."

My daughter would look at me and say, "Mom, that's not the way the teacher says to do it."

There was nothing within that familiar relationship of mother and child that she wanted to learn something new from.

You will find that most immature people do this; so, you may need to get a new life coach. You may need to find someone that can help you embrace truth and bring increase of knowledge, comprehension, understanding, and opportunities. If you want to do new things, I encourage you to invest in yourself.

THE
TAKEAWAY

1. Champions live differently than <u>ordinary people</u>.

2. Winners never quit and <u>quitters</u> never win.

3. The greater the change, the greater the <u>reward</u>.

4. If you want the benefit, there is a <u>procedure</u>.

5. What dreams or goals do you want to achieve?

6. Have you ever wanted to quit something because you felt hurt, confused, and rejected? How did you overcome?

7. Have your dreams and visions been shattered? If so, in what way?

_____

_____

_____

_____

_____

_____

8. How do your priorities align with your vision for life?

_____

_____

_____

_____

_____

9. What does having integrity mean to you?

_____

_____

_____

_____

_____

_____

10. How do you measure one's integrity?

_____

_____

_____

_____

_____

_____

11. What would others say about your integrity?

_____

_____

_____

_____

_____

12. How do you want to influence others?

_____

_____

_____

_____

_____

_____

13.   Do you have the necessary resources and people on
      your team to make your vision a reality?

_____

_____

_____

_____

_____

_____

_____

THE THINGS YOU LEARN IN THE SHALLOWS OF LIFE WILL EQUIP YOU IN THE DEPTHS

_____

ACTION POINTS

1. _____

_____

_____

_____

_____

_____

2. _____

_____

_____

_____

_____

_____

3. _____

_____

_____

_____

_____

_____

4. _____

_____

_____

_____

_____

_____

5. _____

_____

_____

_____

_____

_____

IF YOU DESIRE THE BENEFIT OF
ANYTHING, YOU MUST EMBRACE
THE PROCEDURE NECESSARY TO
MAKE IT YOURS

MEET DR. CLARICE

D r. Clarice Fluitt is a powerful international inspirational speaker, industry leader, author, and popular television personality. As a global trainer for more than four decades, Dr. Fluitt's success is based on her ability to assist organizations and individuals achieve real results. Her experiences as a corporate and executive coach, enterprising businesswoman, and strategic consultant allow her to share her proven strategies for building customer value, inspiring innovation, and generating sustainable growth. Each presentation is crafted and customized to ensure that every audience is equipped with the tools they need to build the kind of champion mindsets that lead to success in today's economy.

Dr. Fluitt has shared the stage with some of the world's most influential leaders in their fields, including Steve Forbes, Suze Orman, Carly Fiorina, Larry King, Michael J. Fox, Rudy Giuliani, Les Brown, Rick Belluzo, Daymond John, Dr. Willie Jolley, Shaquille O'Neal, Joe Montana and other legendary speakers.

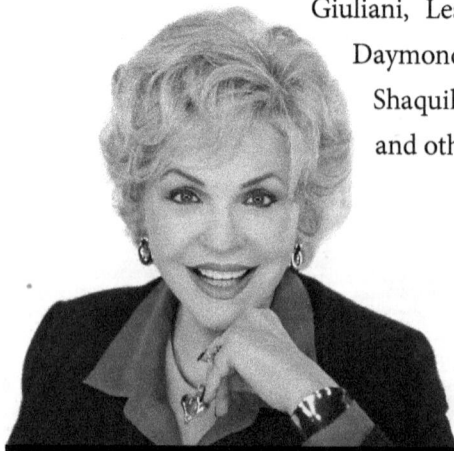

READY FOR REAL RESULTS?

Dr. Clarice is a sought-after master coach because she gets real results and guides you toward real solutions!

Her coaching programs will:

- Help you form fresh open ideas that will launch you from where you are to where you want to be.

- Enhance and enrich your personal development.

- Create a customized, systematic plan to make your goal a reality.

- Focus on your vision.

- Explore the strategies and support structures you need to succeed in reaching your dreams.

Her online coaching programs are designed with solutions in mind and step-by-step strategies for success in outcomes. For more information visit:

_____

WWW.REALRESULTS.SOLUTIONS

_____

CHAMPIONS LIVE
DIFFERENTLY THAN
ORDINARY PEOPLE!

www.ingramcontent.com/pod-product-compliance
Lightning Source LLC
Chambersburg PA
CBHW062026040426
42447CB00010B/2151